Marriage That Survives the Storms

Rev. Simeon Oladokun
Dip. BA (Hons) MA

GW00640769

Zion Publications

Zion Publications
PO Box 4784
London
SE15 6LB

ISBN: 1 874367 78 7

Typeset by CRB Associates, Reepham, Norfolk
Printed in England by Clays Ltd, St Ives plc

Acknowledgements

I give all the glory to our God, the author of marriage and to whom one day we will all give account of how faithful we have been to the vows we made concerning our marriages, for helping me to write this book. I thank Mr Niyi Daramola for sparing the time to read through the manuscripts and make the necessary corrections. I thank my wife, Bola, for her encouragement and support while writing the book. I appreciate all the members of Christ Apostolic Church Mount Zion International for being sources of inspiration. Finally, I value the information derived from many authors whose books are listed in the bibliography.

Contents

Chapter 1

Introduction

According to a report on BBC 1 on Monday 10th February 1997, statistics show that Britain has the highest divorce rate in Europe. It stated that four in ten marriages end in divorce. It also stated that divorce costs the government £4 billion a year in benefits and legal costs. This is only in Britain. In America, divorce is as easy as apple pie. The question is: what went wrong with these marriages? Why couldn't they withstand the storms? Why do they run out of wine? Was marriage made for heart-break or for the happiness of man? Does the author of marriage now take pleasure in the nullification of it? The Psalmist asks in amazement:

> 'When the foundations are being destroyed, what can the righteous do?' (Psalm 11:3)

Foundation is as important in marriage as it is in any stable house.

Hurricane Andrew hit the Southern part of Florida in 1992 and left an estimated $12 billion in damages, 50 people dead and thousands homeless. As a TV news camera crew was filming this devastation, they came to a neighbourhood where all the homes were flattened except for one. The crew went to the owner in the yard and asked him: 'Sir, why is your house the only one still standing? How did you manage to escape the severe damage of the hurricane?' The man replied, 'I built the house myself. I also built it according to the Florida State building code. When the code called for $2' \times 6'$ roof trusses, I used $2' \times 6'$ roof trusses. I was told that a house built according to code could withstand a hurricane. I did, and it did. I suppose no one else around here followed the code.' The institution of marriage has its own code.

Marriage was instituted by God; it was not a human invention, though it has to be worked out by man. It was established in heaven but must be maintained on earth. The fact that it has to be **worked out**, and **maintained** by man, suggests that there will be storms against it; in fact every marriage must be tried by the hurricane of life. Unfortunately many have collapsed today and many still head for the rocks, but this was not the original plan of God for marriage. It was for man's happiness and joy, and to save him from loneliness, for the word of God says:

> 'The Lord God said: "It is not good for the man to be alone..."' (Genesis 2:18)

It also says:

> 'So the man gave names to all the livestock, the birds of the air and all the beasts of the field. **But for Adam no suitable helper was found.**' (Genesis 2:20)

Among the livestock that Adam interacted with I believe, was the horse. Though good for riding and friendly by nature, yet it was not a suitable companion for Adam. Likewise the peacock. When she spread her multi-coloured feathers the man was amazed. But again she was not a suitable companion for him. To make the man happy, and save him from endless loneliness, God had to make a suitable partner for him – Eve, called woman.

The purpose of this book is not just to help people's marriages to survive the unavoidable storms of life, but also to point the people with already broken marriages and those finding married life too tough, to the divine solutions; for I believe that this is the **root of the matter**.

The stories used in this book are real, but to save the persons involved from any embarrassment, I have changed their names.

Chapter 2

Defining Marriage

What is Marriage?

A proper definition of marriage must be given at this juncture, since what constitutes the breaking up of many marriages today, if properly examined, is a wrong conception of what marriage is. Frankly speaking, as popular as the matter of marriage is, and as experienced as many couples are, I realize that many people do not know what marriage really is from biblical point of view. The word of course, remains the same, but its inner world is changing from day to day. The word 'change' is excellent and biblical; after all, Job says,

> '...I will wait until my change comes.' (Job 14:14 KJV)

But unfortunately people tend to change their values and lifestyles; and this contributes significantly to the initial meaning of marriage. People love to experience new things; like the Athenians. Our societies are intoxicated with the love of the 'latest ideas', and surprisingly, a new meaning for marriage has been searched for. In Great Britain today, there is a group that is proposing that the government should allow a ten-year fixed marriage contract instead of a lifetime contract. If it works after ten years, then the couple may renew it. They believe that marriage should be like a car that needs an MOT test (the compulsory annual test of motor vehicles of more than a specified age in the UK), and renewing yearly. If you are fed up with it, then discard it and get another one! What an absurdity. John Stott laments in his comment on the statement of John and Nancy Adam that:

'. . . Letting go of your marriage – if it is no longer good for you – can be the most successful thing you have ever done. Getting a divorce can be a positive, problem-solving, growth-oriented step. It can be a personal triumph.'

John Stott declares:

'Here is the secular mind in all its shameless perversity. It celebrates failure as success, disintegration as growth, and disaster as triumph.'[1]

God does not undertake something he will fail to accomplish. Likewise, he does not want an unsuccessful marriage for us. In the beginning, as stated in Genesis 2:24, the implication is clear – that God instituted an exclusive marriage (it is 'a man and his wife'), the union must be publicly acknowledged ('leaves his parents'), it is a permanent union ('cleaves to his wife'), and consummated by sexual intercourse ('become one flesh'). This then gives us a biblical definition of marriage as:

'. . . an exclusive heterosexual covenant between one man and one woman, ordained and sealed by God, preceded by a public leaving of parents, consummated in sexual union, issuing in a permanent mutually supportive partnership, and normally crowned by the gift of children.'[2]

We will use this definition as a guide throughout this book. Meanwhile, let us first of all consider the 'exclusive' implication of marriage as seen in the above definition. The late Diana Princess of Wales, when interviewed by the BBC in its Panorama programme on 20th November 1995 confirmed the reasons for the breaking down of her marriage. She said: 'There were three of us in this marriage' (i.e. Prince Charles, Diana herself, and Camilla, Prince Charles' lover outside his marriage), 'so it was too crowded.' The reason most peoples' marriages could not survive the storms is that there was no respect for that exclusivity. Marriage by nature, is a union of two, and only two human beings – a man and a woman. And it is only the hands and hearts, souls and bodies of these two that are being united in marriage contract. Anyone and anything that comes in is an intruder and will only make the marriage 'too crowded'.

We note here that the term 'covenant' was used to describe marriage. What is covenant? It is a contract between two partners. In covenantal context, such terms as *to love, solidarity, goodness, friendship, peace, prosperity* and *to serve faithfully in accordance with the covenant* are used. If we do not lose the sense of 'covenant' in our marriage, and hence all these covenantal terms are evident in it, the marriage will survive the storms. But today we have too many convenant breakers. They break the convenants they make with God, and therefore they have no regard whatsoever for any covenant they make with their partners!

The New Bible Dictionary also defines marriage as:

> 'the state in which men and women can live together in sexual relationship with the approval of their social group. Adultery and fornication are sexual relationships that society does not recognize as constituting marriage.'[3]

But it was so sad when we heard the report of the Board of Social Responsibility in the Church of England in June 1995. The study warns against judgmental attitudes towards cohabiting couples and estimates that by the year 2000, four in five will live together before they marry. What the Bible calls sin, is today called 'cohabiting'. In fact the *Sun* newspaper of 7th June 1995 puts in its front page: **'Blessed are those who live in sin'**. But whose children shall they be called? As for our God, he is a holy God and he respects the sacredness of marriage. It is not an institution to make a sinful experiment out of.

References
1. John Stott, *Issues Facing Christians Today*, p. 20
2. John Stott, *Issues Facing Christians Today*, p. 262
3. J.S. Wright, *The New Bible Dictionary*, p. 742

Chapter 3

Seeking for Mr/Miss Right

There is a programme known as *Blind Date* on the ITV (Independent Television, UK) in which a man or woman can ask three men or three women, a few questions without seeing them. The one considered to have best answered the questions will be chosen as partner. They then go on holiday for few days or few weeks to see if they are compatible. For some, it leads to marriage, for others it leads nowhere. Sad to say, some Christians indirectly follow this method of choosing who they should marry. They are children of the God of light, but they go to the market of darkness in search for their Mr/Miss Right without asking God to shed his light on to their feet. There are basic principles to follow when looking for that Mr/Miss Right. Ignoring these principles is often to one's own peril.

Climbing up the Ladder

How well do you know each other?/
The importance of courtship

Wait till you hear the marching sound

Go to Padan-Aram

Commit your way to God

1. Commit your way to God

On climbing up the ladder, the first principle to follow is to commit your way to God. Proverbs says:

> *'Trust in the* LORD *with all your heart and* **lean not on your own understanding;** *in all your ways acknowledge him, and he will make your paths straight.'*
>
> (Proverbs 3:5–6)

The Psalmist also exhorts:

> *'****Commit your way to the*** LORD; *trust in him and he will do this: He will make your righteousness shine like the dawn, the justice of your cause like the noonday sun.'*
>
> (Psalm 37:5–6)

Man is always faced with the temptation to lean on his own understanding; to believe that he knows the thing he/she is looking for. There are millions of daughters of Eve and sons of Adam that are in search for Mr/Miss right. But how do you know which one **is** for you? While engaging on this business, I beseech you friend, do not lean on your own understanding. Samson leaned on his own understanding so he fell into the hands of that woman who is a type of **special agent of darkness – Delilah**. He said to his parents:

> *'... "I have seen a Philistine woman in Timnah; now get her for me as my wife." His father and mother replied, "Isn't there an acceptable woman among your relatives or among all our people? Must you go to the uncircumcised Philistines to get a wife?" But Samson said to his father, "Get her for me.* **She's the right one for me.***" '*
>
> (Judges 14:2–3)

Did Samson involve God in his marriage? No. He simply leaned on his own understanding and eventually met with disappointment. Shouldn't he have learnt by now that he needed to commit his way to the Lord? The Psalmist warns:

> *'Do not be like the horse or the mule, which have no understanding but must be controlled by bit and bridle or they will not come to you.'*   (Psalm 32:9)

Samson is more stubborn than any of these. Often corrected, but falling into the same mistake again and again. Woe unto the day that Samson *'fell in love with a woman in the Valley of Sorek whose name was Delilah'* (Judges 16:4). She was sent with a specific mission, that is, to disorganize Samson's vision as a deliverer, and finally destroy his life. It is a dangerous thing to fall in love with 'Delilah' first before one thinks of committing his/her way to the Lord. This is the mistake that Samson made; and you must spare yourself from falling into the same error. Before anything else, commit your way to God. The flesh may tend to lead you into approaching the wrong partner. You may have even fallen in love with him or her (although you shouldn't by all means). However, because you have committed your way to the Lord and trusted in him rather than leaning on your own understanding, he will save you from falling into a lifetime of trouble; though you may cry sometimes. But it is better to cry for a while than spend all your lifetime crying.

When we say, commit your way to the Lord, we do not mean you should go about seeking a prophet to tell you the mind of God. It is an embarrassment to God that you, his son/daughter should ask someone to speak to him on your behalf. The author of Hebrews says:

> *'Let us then approach the throne of grace with confidence, so that we may receive mercy and find grace to help us in our time of need.'*   (Hebrews 4:16)

And again he says:

> *'Therefore, brothers, since we have confidence to enter the Most Holy Place by the blood of Jesus, by a new and living way opened for us through the curtain that is, his body.'*
> (Hebrews 10:19–20)

If God wants you to come to him and find mercy and grace with regard to your life partner, in your time of need, you should go to him with absolute confidence. Be specific in your prayer, tell God what you want, and let what you want be your song day and night. However, do not allow flesh to dictate for you; let the Holy Spirit be your guide. When you hear a voice in your mind with a great pressure saying: 'Come on, do something, you are getting old; time is against you. Look at your friend Betty, she got married last week. Rebecca also got married two years ago and now has two kids. You are the only odd one out. When would they celebrate with you?' be careful, it may be the devil speaking to you. He wants you to marry just any man outside the will of God. Remember that your God is never in a hurry and so you his child must learn to walk with him in patience. His word exhorts us:

> *'You need to persevere* (have patience) *so that when you have done the will of God, you will receive what he has promised.'*   (Hebrews 10:36)

You will learn more about this in the third step on the ladder.

2. Go to Paddan Aram

When it was time for Isaac to get a wife, Abraham his father called the chief servant in his household and gave him the charge:

> *'I want you to swear by the* Lord, *the God of heaven and the God of earth, that you will not get a wife for my son from the daughters of the Canaanites, among whom I am living, but will go to my country and my own relatives and get a wife for my son Isaac.'*   (Genesis 24:3–4)

> *'Then Rebekah said to Isaac, "I'm disgusted with living because of these Hittite women. If Jacob takes a wife from among the women of this land, from Hittite women like these, my life will not be worth living." So Isaac called for Jacob and blessed him and commanded him: "***Do not marry a Canaanite woman. Go at once to Paddan Aram***, to the house of your mother's father Bethuel. Take wife for yourself there, from among the daughters of Laban, your mother's brother.'*   (Genesis 27:46–28:1–3)

The second step to take while climbing up the ladder is to go to the place we called Paddan Aram which we will explain in a moment. Friend, as you are looking for the person whom you will enjoy the rest of your life with, I beseech you to prayerfully consider this passage. It is the word of God, and forever his word is settled in heaven. Never say 'But this happened in the days of old.' Generations upon generations will pass, but the word of God remains the same. As it was applicable to the people of old, so it is to you and me.

It is a common thing nowadays for Christian brothers and sisters to say that it doesn't matter who they marry, whether a Christian or not, born again or unregenerated, they can change the person later. This is a grievous mistake. A man who is ignorant of the fact that you were created an image of God will not treat you as God's image; he will enslave you, ill-treat you, and deform God's image in you. Likewise, a woman who has not been led to Christ cannot be led by a husband. In other words, when the Bible exhorts the wives to submit to their own husbands, we should not expect a woman who has not submitted herself to Christ to submit herself to any man. Can you see the problem then? You may argue, what about Joseph who married an Egyptian, didn't it work out well for him? What about Mahlon and Kilion the children of Naomi who married Moabite women, Orpah and Ruth? Didn't Ruth turn out to be a woman of noble character, putting her faith in the God of Israel? And perhaps many more. Yes, you are right. In a place like the land of Israel of old, which was a theocratic state, where no other faith was permitted except Yahwism (worship of Jehovah alone) it was easier. The unbelieving partner would have no choice other than to worship Yahweh/Jehovah your God with you. Even so it was still dangerous, hence, the Lord warned his people never to intermarry with the people of Canaan. A Canaanite woman or man may be gentle, and generous, having a sense of understanding and perhaps possessing some moral qualities; but nothing can be substituted for salvation.

History has proved it, experience confirms it, that

marriage was never meant to be a means or vehicle for conversion. You may believe that you will change your unbelieving partner, but you may be surprised that it is you that has to change. The odds are against you. If you go into partnership with a man who is in a pit, you are at a disadvantage. The Law of Gravity is in his favour. Jesus bids us to *'Remember Lot's wife'* (Luke 17:32). There is a lot to remember about that woman which we cannot mention in this book for lack of space, but there are a few points that we must notice here. Do you remember that she was not an Israelite? She may have been a native of Sodom or perhaps an Egyptian woman, or a Canaanite. With all her association with righteous Lot, she could still not tear herself away from the love of Sodom. A flight without so much as looking back was demanded of her, but this was too much, hence she perished. But let us also remember Lot himself. I think when he got married, his wife assumed the ruling place and guided the way of his life. To a certain extent, he had been badly influenced by his wife. His daughters as well became so immoral.

Another example is that of King Solomon. The most prudent of all the kings of Israel, and yet the most foolish king that had ever lived. Why? The Bible answers:

> '[he] *loved **many foreign women** besides Pharaoh's daughter Moabites, Ammonites, Edomites, Sidonians and Hittites. They were from nations about which the* LORD *had told the Israelites, "You must not intermarry with them ... "'* (1 Kings 11:1–2)

Do you notice that polygamy was not the only cause of Solomon's downfall? It was also his marriages with unconverted, or unregenerated women. Friend, go to 'Paddan Aram', to your people, the people purchased by the precious blood of Jesus as you were. They are your people, that is your 'Paddan Aram'. If you can't get a partner for yourself in your local church, go to another Bible-based church (this is not advice to leave your church). You cannot finish travelling to all the houses of the family of God before you meet that man/woman.

If you get married to an incompatible partner, in some

areas you could make adjustments. But please, never play with this area of choosing in the Lord. If your partner is an unbeliever, you do not have the same controller. You are being controlled by the Holy Spirit, but he/she is in the world, and Satan is called the prince of this world. Therefore, you two are bound to go in opposite directions. Your Controller says 'You must not commit adultery,' but his/her own controller has no 'adultery' in his dictionary. He is permitted to cheat on his partner, but you are not. Your own Controller says 'be sincere with one another,' but there is no sincerity in Satan. He is a liar from the beginning, so those he governs have to lie too. How dare you tell him/her not to smoke or drink alcohol? Is he/she a temple of God such as you are? You lay up treasures for yourself in heaven, but he/she loves the world and so cares for it. Prophet Amos asks:

> *'Do two walk together unless they have agreed to do so?'*
> (Amos 3:3)

What agreement do you have with such a person? Have you considered the fact that the implication of this passage in Amos is that unless you and your partner are in total agreement concerning your marriage, you will never reach the same destination? If you are northbound, he/she will be southbound; if you go eastbound, he/she may go west. Can you then reach the same destination? You will walk by faith (2 Corinthians 5:7) he/she will walk by sight. Where you need to take a step of faith in your marital life, he/she will say, 'Dear, don't be silly, that won't work; I won't be a party to that.' Would there be any progress then in your life? Please,

> *'Do not be yoked together with unbelievers. For what do righteousness and wickedness have in common? Or what fellowship can light have with darkness? What harmony is there between Christ and Belial? What does a believer have in common with an unbeliever?'*
> (2 Corinthians 6:14–15)

Having said this however, we realize that some brethren have fallen into this great mistake already, and it is our encouragement that they need. For this reason, we shall return to this issue later on.

3. Wait till you Hear the Marching Sound

Now you know that looking for the right partner outside the church of God is not advisable. It is a terrible mistake that one must avoid by all means. Moreover, you are now looking in the church, be it in your own local church or anywhere else in Christendom. Thank God you have finally found one. What is the next step? The Psalmist says:

> *'For this God is our God for ever and ever; **he will be our guide even to the end**.'* (Psalm 48:14)

The Lord who has been your guide from day one of your journey until now is so interested in guiding you on 'even to the end.' He does not do his work halfheartedly. But there is a lesson for you here, Friend: that is a lesson of **waiting**. The Pilot must wait and not take off or land until he is instructed to do so from the control tower. The driver has studied in his Highway Code that when the traffic light is red, he/she must wait until it turns green. Likewise the soldier must wait for the signal from the commander before approaching the enemies. This was what David did when the Philistines went in full force to fight with him in the Valley of Rephaim. The first time, the Bible says:

> *'So David enquired of the LORD, "Shall I go and attack the Philistines? Will you hand them over to me?" The LORD answered him, "Go, for I will surely hand the Philistines over to you."'* (2 Samuel 5:19)

This time, David defeated his enemies for the Lord had broken out against his enemies before him as waters break out. But the stubborn Philistines came back again. David did not say, well, I enquired of the Lord earlier, and he answered 'Yes', therefore I do not need to enquire of him again. No, he needed a new instruction. The directive of yesterday had gone with yesterday. Master what do you say today? Shall I go just as I did before? Surprisingly, the Lord answered:

> ' . . . *"Do not go straight up, but circle round behind them and attack them in front of the balsam trees. As soon as you hear the sound of marching in the tops of the balsam trees, move quickly, because that will mean the* LORD *has gone out in front of you to strike the Philistine army."* '
>
> (2 Samuel 5:22–24)

Can you see the benefit of consulting God before one makes any move? Can you also see that God is not limited to only one method? That is why we must constantly seek his face in all our undertakings, especially in this area of choosing a life partner.

Apostle Paul affirms that:

> ' . . . *Satan himself masquerades as an angel of light.*'
>
> (2 Corinthians 11:14)

In this book we have been warning the children of God of the danger of marrying to an unbeliever, but attention needs to be paid to those false brothers and sisters in the church. We must expose them to save the innocent brothers and sisters from falling into their traps. To do this, we shall choose a character in the Bible to illustrate our points. That character is **Amnon, a type of carnal Christian**. His love affair, or rather 'lust affair' with Princess Tamar has something to say to any Christian brother or sister that may be looking for a partner or may have found one, even in the church of God. His name 'Amnon' means 'faithful'. But his beastly nature betrayed his fair name. He was also a carnal man and the language he used when he wanted to rape Tamar suggests this. Let us quickly turn to the passage, 2 Samuel 13:6 and please, carefully look at the words emphasized:

> 'So Amnon **lay down** and **pretended** to be ill. When the king came to see him, Amnon said to him, "I would like my sister Tamar to come and make some **special bread** in my sight, so that **I may eat from her hand**."'

He laid down as lion lays down in wait for its prey. He

pretended, as the carnal Christians do when they suspend all their ungodly habits and pretend to be born again Christians until our innocent Tamars fall into their traps in marriage.

A little more explanation on Amnon's initial request will show him clearly as the typical carnal man he was. In verse six of that passage, he initially requested 'some special bread'. The Moffatt translation says:

> '...come, and make one or two cakes, **the shape of a heart**, before my eyes.'

The Hebrew word he used for the kind of cake he wanted was derived from Hebrew word *lebab* meaning 'heart', a clue for David and Tamar as to what this man was really up to.

This man was also sensual in his speech. In verse 11 he said to Tamar, *'Come to bed with me, my sister.'* This is a figurative speech meaning 'my beloved, or my lover' as it is in (Songs of Songs 5:1). Being a carnal and sensual man, he eventually robbed Tamar of her beauty, her pride and glory, then he hated her. But note that with all these evil characteristics, he was still living in the palace. What a picture of the carnal Christians we have been discussing. They speak to you lovingly as dear brother and sister, but please, never follow them into their inner chamber as Tamar did. They often 'prevail' in there. You have no future with such a person, he/she only comes to rob you of your princely glory. Therefore, child of God, don't be naive in concluding that the brother/sister that has started dating you is **an open door**. He/she may be **an open trap**. So you need discerning eyes to distinguish between the two, as there are so many 'Amnons' in the palace of the king, waiting for 'Tamars' to defile. But if you wait until you hear the marching sound, you will save yourself from falling into their traps. Sometimes you may feel that your waiting period is so long. That is because flesh hates waiting; it wants action. But as you are waiting, you are learning. Since God is teaching you something during your waiting period, you are not losing. As a child of God, you trust God, but test people. That is scriptural. Listen to what the Bible says:

> '*Remember how the* LORD *your God led you all the way in the desert these forty years, to humble you and* **to test you in order to know what was in your heart . . .** '
>
> (Deuteronomy 8:2)

Motives are not easily discerned and the wrong people can keep their motives covered for a long time, but waiting forces the truth to surface. Your waiting will reveal what is in the heart of that person you are dating.

4. How well do you know each other?/ The importance of courtship

Like the former three steps, this step on the ladder is very crucial as well for a marriage that will survive the storms of life. I believe that most people will hope to have a relationship that is based on love, but one must understand that the love that will make marriage a lasting one may not come all at once but in stages. How the two of you first met, and the kind of situations in which you normally see each other, will make a difference to your perception of each other. So this stage in the steps that lead to marriage is important, particularly in our present generation where faithfulness and sincerity mean nothing to many people.

We are often told that prevention is better than cure. Never is that more true than in the area of marriage. Child of God, never be rushed into marriage. If you rush into it, you may soon have to rush out of it. It is God that provides the one you will marry for you, but God will not tell you when to go to the altar with him/her. He wants you to know the person you are marrying quite well.

One day as I was counselling George and Caroline (not their real names) the former broke out in tears and said: 'Carol, do you remember I told you to let us wait for some time before we entered into this? But you wouldn't listen. You said we either wed now or you would quit.' 'Pastor,' he turned to me, 'I've been going through hell since we married.' Unfortunately, Caroline knew quite well that it wouldn't take long for her strange characteristics to be detected should they court each other for a while. Hence she insisted on going to a registry office for their wedding.

You must not be afraid of what will be uncovered in the nature of the person you are courting. It is true to say that a broken engagement is better than a broken marriage. There are hundreds of questions you need to address before the D-day. You need to know whether or not you are quite satisfied with the answers you've got to such questions as:

- How does your fiancé/fiancée behave under stress?
- Is he/she emotionally stable?
- What is something you do that really makes him/her unhappy and how does he/she react to that?
- What does he/she like to do more than anything else?
- Do you have any reservation about how he/she is dealing with money?
- Are you financially able to go into marriage?
- Is he industrious?
- Does he work or is he a man that will turn marriage into slavery for you?
- Have you seen how he/she reacts to the situation in emergencies?
- Yes, you've heard the statement, 'I love you' from him/her several times before, but ask yourself as things are going between the two of you, is it true or too good to be true?
- Have you two come to any agreement on the cultural, educational or perhaps social differences between you?
- Does an age gap matter to any of you?
- If you will be the wife, do you plan to be a full-time housewife or you will want to work, and what is his opinion on that?
- Has he/she been married before? If so, what led to the break-up and will that create problems in this marriage?
- If the children from the former marriage will be in this new home, what steps will you have to take to make them feel accepted and wanted?

- Does he/she possess any unhelpful habit?
- Do you realize the fact that marriage is not a reform school and that the ceremony itself will do nothing to change such habit?

Such questions, and many more, should be addressed during the courtship. In courtship 95% of things go well. But in the 5% of things that go wrong you get the real thing. It is here you often know the real man/woman you are marrying.

Moreover, the time of courtship is not a time to be too optimistic about one another; nor a time to be naive. It is a time to attempt to know whether one's partner is a robin friend or a swallow one; Spurgeon said:

> 'I would rather have a robin for a friend than a swallow; for a swallow abides with us only in the summer time, but a robin comes to us in the winter.'

In other words, a partner who stays firmly with you in winter time will last; while your fair-weather fiancé/fiancée will soon flee away. Think deeply about it.

However, you must realize you cannot know everything about the person you are courting. That is why Jeremiah declares:

> '*The heart is deceitful above all things and beyond cure. Who can understand it? I the* LORD *search the heart and examine the mind . . .*'   (Jeremiah 17:9–10)

Having therefore, known as much as the Lord your God has helped you to know about him/her, it is then time to begin to take possession of what the Lord has given you.

Chapter 4

The Pillars of the Marriage that Survives the Storms

I do believe that every couple hopes for a marriage that will last and as I have noted earlier, God did not institute marriage in order to bring unhappiness and sorrow to man; quite the opposite. However, we must understand again the fact that marriage was designed in heaven but has to be worked out on earth. To make it work therefore, each party in the marriage should prayerfully consider these subjects that we call pillars; for with them being the pillars on which you build your matrimonial home, you will laugh at the storms when they blow at your marriage.

A. Love

The word, 'love' sounds simple and the letters in it also look simple. Unfortunately, when it comes to defining what it really means, it becomes problematic, for it means different things to different people. Sadly, what many people call love, isn't love at all. We will therefore endeavour to give as many meanings as we can get until we finally arrive at the most satisfactory one.

What is love?

The Oxford English Dictionary takes five pages to define love without much success even after all that effort. As I have implied earlier, if we ask a hundred people for a definition of love, it is quite possible to get at least ninety different answers. The reason is that the world has no clear-cut definition of love. Meanings are given according to individual experiences and viewpoints. Love can be passion, affection, romantic feelings, friendship, fondness, infatuation, or innumerable combinations of those qualities. One thing that is common in whatever definition people give, is the expectation of getting something in return. This idea of 'getting', 'getting' and 'getting' in love will be elaborated on in due course. The New Bible Dictionary defines love as follows:

> 'In the Old Testament love, whether human or divine, is the deepest possible expression of the personality and of the closeness of personal relations.' [It continues] '... Fundamentally it is an inner force ... which impels to performing the action which gives pleasure ... obtaining the object which awakens desire ... or in the case of persons to self-sacrifice for the good of the loved one ... and unswerving loyalty ...' [1]

One thing I love most in the above definition is the fact that love is **an inner force**. It drives you to do something, to express something, to give something, to sacrifice something, and to demonstrate loyalty. Thus Mary Batchelor comments on love:

> 'The love that is adequate for a successful marriage must contain the full spectrum of meanings which includes:
> – **Sexual attraction** – a very important ingredient of married love,
> – **Affection** – which helps a couple to put up with each other's quirks and foibles with tolerance and humour,
> – **Friendship** – supposes shared interests and viewpoints or a willingness to share the other's interests ... it remains constant when passion fluctuates ...,
> – **Respect** – *When the first impressions prove to be a mere deception* and someone who seemed out of this world now turns out to be only too human and full of faults, respect keeps failings private and on the positive side continues to recognize the other's intrinsic worth, (and)

- **Romance** – which is based on the excitement of the differences between man and woman and includes treating the other as still mysterious, unattainable and special, even after years of marriage! It makes marriage more than merely a sensible agreement for living together and enjoying each other's company.'[2]

Mary is absolutely right. But there is more to say on love in the marriage. Let us turn to that right now.

Love in marriage

Repetitive aspect
For love to be a strong pillar of a matrimonial home, it has to be repetitive. One of my favourite passages of the Scripture is Hosea 3:1:

> 'The LORD said to me, "Go, show your love to your wife **again**, though she is loved by another and is an adulteress. Love her as the LORD loves the Israelites, though they turn to other gods and love the sacred raisin cakes." '

Can you see the word 'again' in the text? In fact, the verb 'love' is the dominating vocabulary of this verse. It occurs five times there. We may ask, what is the sense of it? The answer is, it includes divine love (*agape*), parental love (*storge*), general human social love (*philos*), and romantic love (*heros*). For prophet Hosea to show the greatness of Yahweh's love for Israel (the love that cannot accept rejection as final) therefore, he must show his love for this adulterous woman in all these areas.

Your love for your partner will surely be tested by his/her faults. At that time, remember the words 'show your love again.'

> 'Love covers a multitude of sins.'   (1 Peter 4:8)

Exclusive aspect
Remember that we have said something about this before when we were giving definition of marriage. For both husband and wife, love must be exclusive. There is a mentality in our society. While most couples believe that

unfaithfulness in marriage is not good, there are many who are bailing out of marriage instead of working through their problems. Having divorced, they then turn around and marry someone else, hoping that a new person can meet their needs. What this really represents is serial polygamy. Even though someone might be faithful to the one he marries, that 'one' keeps changing. Henry Ford was once asked of the secret of his long and apparently happy marriage. His reply was, 'I follow the same principle in marriage that I do in business – I stick with one model.' How beautiful it would be if everyone could follow this advice – 'sticking with one model'.

Giver or getter?

Our society is characterized with 'give and take' attitude. Such selfish practice has no room in a home marked by the *agape* love. In marriage we can be either 'a giver' or 'a getter'. Givers delight to meet the needs of their partner, while getters are more concerned about having their own needs met. A preacher has rightly put it: 'You can give without loving, but you can't love without giving.' Love is about giving, but not giving just anything, after all, what you do no longer need in your home is better given away. But it is about giving your best. Love is proved by what it prompts to give. The Bible says:

> 'For God so loved the world that he gave his one and only Son . . . '   (John 3:16)

God didn't give one son out of many, but he gave his only Son. Moreover, not just his only Son, but a beloved Son; he said:

> ' . . . This is my Son, whom I love; with him I am well pleased.'   (Matthew 3:17)

Let me sum this heading up with the words of Ed and Gaye Wheat:

> 'Love, in essence, is that deliberate act of giving one's self to another so that the other person constantly receives enjoyment. Love gives, and love's richest

reward comes when the object of love responds to the gift of one's self.'[3]

This is particularly true of the husband when he sees himself as the lover and the giver in the home.

B. *Commitment*

If you ask me who is the strongest man in the world, I will say it is the committed man. A committed man is a consecrated person, and a consecrated person is a strong man indeed. In the Roman wars with Phrrhus, there was an oracle which said that victory would attend that army whose leader should give himself up to death. Decius, the Roman Consul, knowing this rushed into the thick of the battle that his army might overcome by his dying. This proved his commitment. Every Roman man at that time seemed to be a hero because every man was a consecrated or committed man. They went to battle with this thought:

> 'I will conquer or die; the name Rome is written on my heart; for my country I am prepared to live, or for that to shed my blood.'

No enemies could ever stand against them. If a Roman fell, there were no wounds in his back, but all in his breast. His face even in cold death was like the face of a lion. They were men committed to their country. They were ambitious to make the name of Rome the noblest word in the human language; and consequently Rome became a giant. Can you see what you will make of your marriage if both of you can be committed? There is no area of life that commitment does not play an essential role. As the soldiers and the business people need it, so do the students, and also the professionals. Commitment is vital for the stability of your marriage. Listen to what Ed and Gaye Wheat say on this subject:

> 'With today's come-and-go marriages, total commitment would seem to be out of date. But perhaps we have allowed the world to set our expectations for us, making divorce the norm instead of the exception.

There are permanent; but with a 50 percent divorce rate in parts of our nation, some of those people have failed somewhere. Perhaps part of the problem is a lack of commitment to commitment!'[4]

Think deeply over the statement of our Lord Jesus on marriage:

> *'Therefore what God has joined together, let man not separate.'*   (Mark 10:9)

This needs to become such a part of our thinking that full commitment to marriage, no matter what, will be our only option. In other words, when we go into marriage it should be with the conviction **that there is no way out**. Then you and your partner will be committed to making the marriage a success. May I tell you that marriage does not necessarily make people happy. But people can make their marriage a happy one by giving to one another, working together, serving together, and growing together.

C. *Communication*

One of the quickest ways in which Satan destroys many matrimonial homes is the lack of proper communication. Selwyn Hughes quoted a man who was boasting (ignorantly) before the counsellor:

> ' "We have never had an argument in the whole of our marriage," said the husband. "How did you accomplish that?" asked the counsellor. "We just don't talk." '[5]

Funny as it may be, it is sad that many couples do find communicating with each other extremely difficult. Some men do love their wives sincerely. They are good husbands but poor communicators. Likewise many women are angry about the attitudes of their husbands, but they have a poor way of showing it. As a result Satan has taken advantages of these loopholes in their marriages. When I said poor communicators, I mean that it is possible not to communicate. Speaking, on its own, is not communication. Whether we choose to speak or not to speak, our faces go on 'speaking' with scores of readily identifiable signals. Somebody has said that **communication answers questions: Who says what? In what manner? To whom? With what effect?** For a marriage to be a happy one, the couple must have time to think through the questions.

Selwyn Hughes in his book, *Marriage as God Intended*, has brilliantly divided the communication process into three principles, namely **talking**, **listening**, and **understanding**. I will summarize them here but for a fuller treatment of it, I recommend you get a copy of the book.

Talking

Talking is not just the opposite of silence, neither is talking for the sake of talking good communication. However, talking with point and purpose is an essential ingredient of effective communication. This is a general rule. But for a Christian couple, merely talking isn't enough; you must talk out your problems in love. This is what the Bible exhorts us to do – '...*speaking the truth in love*...' (Ephesians 4:15). When you speak out your mind, it means you talk things out rather than withdrawing into silence. In initiating a good conversation, ask your partner questions, especially those that cause him/her to pour out his/her mind. Questions are to a good marriage relationship what food is to living. Note that the apostles said the truth must be spoken **in love**. The truth that is told with sarcasm, accusations and name-calling isn't truth at all. Job asks *'is there flavour in the white of an egg?'* (Job 6:6). Be careful as to the words you use to speak out the truth, but also consider the tone of your voice. If you are wrong about a matter, say 'sorry' and mean it. Some people find it almost impossible to say 'sorry'. They may show that they want to make it up but they cannot bring themselves to utter the words, 'I'm sorry, I was wrong.' To admit to being wrong and to ask forgiveness calls for maturity, humility and enough confidence to know that the world won't collapse because you've made a mistake.

Listening

A gentleman kept on saying to his wife as their marriage was facing the storms: 'At least let's sit down and talk for God's sake.' 'There is nothing to talk about,' said the wife. The man eventually withdrew into silence, but even this didn't satisfy the wife as she felt uneasy living under the same roof with the man without knowing what he was up to. On a different note, a lady once told me with regret that she is not allowed by her husband to say she has something to discuss with him. In communication between husband and wife Peter Cotterell said that:

> 'The most vital factor is not talking but **listening**. Listening to what is being said, listening to what is no longer being said, listening even when she blows her top and says a lot of things of which afterwards she professes to be heartily ashamed.'[6]

For your marriage to survive the blows of the storms, learn to listen. In the process of this, first of all try to recognize the obstacles that prevent you from effective listening and work on removing them. For example, the obstacle could be defensiveness. All that you often think about when things get hot between the two of you, is the reason why you believe he is wrong and you are right. It is an obstacle to a proper way of listening.

Another obstacle to effective listening is self-centredness or self-preoccupation. If you are characterized with interrupting your partner's conversations thereby preventing him/her from completing what he/she is saying; check it. You aren't a good listener.

It is also vitally important to repeat to the other person precisely what you have heard him/her say. Communication between one person and another is often distorted without one or both persons knowing it. The husband may say something and the wife takes it wrongly for that is how she had understood it. But when we restate to another person what we have heard them say, we give them the chance to confirm or deny the accuracy of what we have understood them to say. In other words, say to your partner, 'This is what I said,' or 'this is what I meant,' and that settles the matter. Learn to listen. It can bring about a transformation in your marriage.

Understanding

Missildine is right in saying that there are six people in every marriage bed. The husband and wife, the father and mother of the husband and the father and mother of the wife. People often say of their partners, 'I just can't understand why he/she behaves like that.' It is a big enough problem to endeavour to understand the behaviour of a single human-being; how much more when the two persons in marriage bring in their backgrounds. There is an old saying that to understand all is to forgive all, and nowhere is that more true than in marriage. When your wife or husband behaves in ways that cause you some irritation, make a deliberate effort to try to understand what causes them to behave in the way they do. All behaviour is caused, say the psychologists and they are right. There are reasons why we behave the way we do. Remember each has his/her own background and environment, and we bring these into marriage relationship.

D. Consideration

It is an attribute of God to consider the nature of his creatures. Concerning the Israelites in the wilderness, the Psalmist says:

> *'He remembered that they were but flesh, a passing breeze that does not return.'*   (Psalm 78:39)

Over and over again the Israelites sinned against God in the desert, but God in his mercy forgave their iniquities, simply because he considered their nature. He considered what they were made of and hence he 'handled them with care.' This is how God who made us treats us. Now listen,

> *'You are all sons* (and daughters) *of God through faith in Christ Jesus.'*   (Galatians 3:26)

If God is our Father, we imitate his nature. Listen again:

> *'Be imitators of God, therefore, as dearly loved children.'*
>
> (Ephesians 5:1)

and again,

> *' ... he has given us his very great and precious promises, so that through them you may **participate in the divine nature** ... '*   (2 Peter 1:4)

As a child of God therefore, share in the nature of God, and be considerate towards one another just as God considers our weaknesses. Husbands in particular, see what God commands you to do:

> *'Husbands, in the same way **be considerate** as you live with your wives, and treat them with respect as the weaker partner and as heirs with you of the gracious gift of life, so that nothing will hinder your prayers.'*   (1 Peter 3:7)

Don't compare your wife with somebody else's wife. She is what she is; neither model your marriage on another marriage that seems ideal. Remember that every marriage is different.

E. Planning Together

Prophet Amos asks:

> *'Do two walk together unless they have agreed to do so?'*
>
> (Amos 3:3)

It is surprising to know that when many couples are thinking of going into marriage, they do not sit down to address the issue of planning together the sort of shape they wish their marriage to take; whether they wish to share **everything** together; that is, material things, or they prefer to opt for 'what's mine's my own' attitude.

Interestingly, as I was starting to write this part of the book, Sarah and Joel (not their real names) came to me for counselling. The wife came first and claimed that her marriage was about to end. I asked the reason for this and she replied that her husband was planning to leave both her and their children. I made the request to see both of them and thank God, he touched the heart of the man, and he and his wife came to see me. According to them, many people including Sarah, had wanted to know why the man intended to end the relationship after ten years, but he had refused to tell anyone. But after asking him a few questions he opened up and said that his wife was too selfish, building up a future for herself alone. Financially, he did not know what his wife earned; whereas, she knew everything about his. The wife was planning to buy a house on the grounds that things might not work out for them. This was without the knowledge of her husband. In the first place, Sarah and Joel did not have any positive attitude towards their marriage. There was always the feeling that things would go wrong one day. And as nobody wanted to be the loser, the wife decided to take pre-emptive actions to protect herself.

Students of the mind are discovering that a person never rises above his expectations. When a person anticipates failure, he will never succeed. If, however, he expects success, he will achieve it. Sarah concentrated so much on failure rather than success. Coupled with this, the element of trust was lacking in their home. They did not trust each other. Whatever the wife heard about her husband from outside she believed it and likewise, the husband. Words that are spoken in anger are taken at their face value. In short, there was no trust whatsoever in the home and this had undermined their love for one another.

As the lack of trust undermines love in the home, so also we must say that it doesn't help the marriage relationship when the partners think, and act, negatively towards their marriage relationship. Remember that it is a life contract. It is a '**permanent mutually supportive partnership**,' as stated in the definition of marriage. If so, why think negatively? Did you join yourselves together in order to live separately as time goes by? It was said that 'the two shall become one': one in spirit, soul and body. But shouldn't they be one in material things as well? What belongs to the husband, shouldn't the wife be able to claim it with boldness? Your marriage is a type of the union between Christ and his Church. Now, whatever belongs to Christ rightly becomes the Church's. For the Scripture says:

> '...*All things are yours, whether Paul or Apollos or Cephas or the world or life or death or the present or the future – all are yours, and you are of Christ and Christ is of God.'*   (1 Corinthians 3:21–23)

Would Christ build a future for himself and not concern the Church? Would it be right for the Church to be thinking selfishly of herself and not of Christ her husband, and head? If not, then, the couples who have allowed this spirit of selfishness in their midst should think again and make adjustments.

One home, one purse?

The question we are addressing here is 'Should the husband and wife have a joint account or a separate account?' To answer this question we need to ask another question: How many bank accounts do they want to have? Just one, two or even three or more? Couples are different. Many people, even though they believe in sharing their money, like to have separate accounts. This will help them for example to buy surprise gifts for their partners at any time. But the fear of many goes farther than that. What if your partner is the type who spends money lavishly? Or what advice can we give to a person like Rosemary (not her real name) who had everything in common with her partner but landed on her husband's debt after their marriage had broken down? Or Florence (not her real name) who is a born again Christian but has an unbelieving husband who doesn't permit her to pay any tithe or other offerings to the Church. Yet they have a joint account which he controls. I will therefore say that, while I favour a joint account, and believe it to be the best for a couple since it reinforces the trust in marriage, every marriage is different. Whatever method is most suitable to your relationship has to be adopted. Julie Reeves' comment is very helpful here. She writes:

'...the important thing is not how many bank accounts you choose to have, but your attitude to what goes into them.'[7]

F. Praying Together

> '...apart from me you can do nothing.'   (John 15:5)

I believe that every reasonable couple expects to have a healthy and stable home. But this doesn't just happen automatically. It needs to be fought for. For your home to be a happy, stable, and healthy home, you need to engage in a sort of spiritual warfare. I deliberately used this term 'spiritual warfare' to show that there is a force that tirelessly opposes Christian homes.

An American minister of God was preaching some time ago and he said that when he was in the plane the crew served food the first time, but the woman sitting beside him refused to take it. The samething happened the second and the third times. Then he curiously asked her, 'lady are you fasting?' 'Yes,' she replied. The man of God was so naive that he presumed she must be a Christian. 'Are you a Christian?' he asked. The woman replied emphatically: 'No, I worship Satan and the reason we are fasting is to trouble the Christian homes. When they have trouble in their homes they will not be able to concentrate on their mission.'

This may sound funny and incredible, but sometimes when you listen to couples who are quarrelling you are often puzzled as to the real sources of their fight. Satan is the arch-enemy of God and of God's works including marriage. It is surprising that many couples are so busy with their works and other things that they neglect prayer and the study of the word of God. They forget that there is a force that is parading around their home in order to plant the seed of bitterness in there. The Bible says,

> 'But while everyone was sleeping, his enemy came and sowed weeds among the wheat, and went away.'
>
> (Matthew 13:25)

You care so much about your business and academic life but the pillars that could hold your matrimonial home you have no time for. Listen to these:

> '... Man does not live on bread alone, but on every word that comes from the mouth of God.'   (Matthew 4:4)

> 'Let the word of Christ dwell in you richly as you teach and admonish one another with all wisdom and as you sing psalms, hymns and spiritual songs with gratitude in your hearts to God.'   (Colossians 3:16)

Can you see from these passages what the family devotion is all about? Can you see prayer and the study of the word of God in there? Build your home life around this and it will lead to more happiness and harmony in your home. Remember the parable of that man of God who was sent to rebuke Ahab. The parable tells of a soldier who was given a captive to be watched and was instructed as follows:

> '... Guard this man. If he is missing, it will be your life for his life, or you must pay a talent of silver. While your servant was busy here and there, the man disappeared...'
> (1 Kings 20:39–40)

You too have been instructed to guard your marriage against any external force; any evil force. So you need to be vigilant in prayer and study of the word of God. Should you be *'so busy here and there,'* that you neglect your duty, there is always a heavy price to pay when you carelessly allow your marriage to come to ruins.

G. *Your Role, My Role*

God is a God of order. In the beginning orderliness took priority as he began his creative works in the universe that was enveloped in total darkness. Apostle Paul testifies to this by saying:

> 'For God is not a God of disorder but of peace.'
> (1 Corinthians 14:33)

Our society today is intoxicated with many liberation movements – women, gays, and ethnic minorities. Not all these fights could be condemned as wrong, but the fact that this mentality has found its way into the marriage institution bringing its horrible effects on many homes, is very alarming. The author of peace has designed roles that are suitable for each partner in the marriage. The problem, however, is that the wife wants to take over her husband's role, and the children are struggling to take the place assigned to the parents. Thus, we see the reversal of the whole system. But in the home where the scriptural guidelines are followed, there will be peace and harmony, not confusion and disintegration. Such family will withstand any storm that might beat against it.

The wife's role

As we have mentioned, God has a perfect order for the husband and wife in marriage. This order is found in Ephesians 5:22–33.

> *'Wives submit to your husbands as to the Lord ... Now as the church submits to Christ, so also wives should submit to their husbands in everything.'*   (Ephesians 5:22, 24)

Some Christian women look at this statement with total dissatisfaction. They believe it is very humiliating and insulting and for this reason when exchanging marriage vows, some of these women omit the word 'obey'. But that is when one fails to understand the true sense of the word 'submission' here. It does not make the wife a doormat, neither does it make her subject to a cruel and insensitive husband who rules his family with a rod of iron. In fact, there are two things to be clarified here immediately.

First, do you notice that in asking the wife to submit to her own husband, the Bible does not use the word 'obey'? This is in reference to the children and the slaves in chapter six verses one and five. But it uses the word 'submit' for the wife, which means voluntarily yielding one's own rights or will.

Secondly, do you notice that it has occurred in the previous verse in this context? There it says:

'Submit to one another out of reverence for Christ.'

In the Greek, the verb 'to submit' (*hupotasso*) does not appear at all in verse 22 but the verb was borrowed from verse 21. This shows that the section on marriage doesn't start with verse 22 but with verse 21 and introduces the whole subject by the requirement that we should submit to one another, that is, wife and husband alike.

Having said this however, the fact that in God's perfect order, the man is the head is clear. And being the head, he should be in charge and the wife should happily take the place of subordination. Do not allow a 'power struggle' in your home or take your man as a sort of 'figure-head husband'. It is an act of rebellion and arrogance, not only against your husband, but also against God who instituted marriage. Rebellion, Samuel said *'is like the sin of divination and arrogance like the evil of idolatry . . . '* (1 Samuel 15:23). Some women are like Jezebel, Ahab's wife. They are in charge of decision-making. All that they need is their husband's stamp. That's OK with Jezebel, the forceful and self-willed daughter of Ethbaal, but not for you, a daughter of the Lord God Most High.

A Spanish proverb says:

> 'Woe to the house where the hen crows and the cock keeps quiet.'

Selwyn Hughes also once quoted a woman who declared:

> 'I don't mind my husband being the head as long as I can be the neck and turn him whichever way I want him to go!' [8]

What folly!

When the Bible says you should submit yourself to your own husband, it means you should let him have the final decision on every matter. That doesn't mean that your own opinion is not counted here as we shall soon see. If he loves you, he will value your opinion. But leave the matter with him to decide. Let him be the leader and you and the children be the followers. I love the name the wife of C.H. Spurgeon called her husband – 'governor'. It is because she has given him all the leadership roles. As Woodrow Kroll rightly puts it:

> 'The greatest gift a wife can give her husband is the right to be the leader of the home as God meant him to be. Sure he'll make mistakes. Everyone does. But being disobedient to God's will is the biggest mistake of all.' [9]

Secondly, give the due respect to your husband. The Bible's command is:

> *'Give every one what you owe him: If you owe taxes, pay taxes, if revenue, then revenue; if respect, then respect; if honour, then honour.'*   (Romans 13:7)

If the due respect has to be given to the government authorities simply because they were ordained by God; and failure to do so is consequently regarded as rebelling against what God has instituted (verse 2), how much more should you give the respect and honour due to the husband God himself has given you?

In the third place, in submitting yourself to your own husband, you have security. God has mysteriously hidden your protection and security in your husband: security from any external pressure. It takes all unnecessary loads off you. On the contrary if you assume the responsibilities your husband has neglected, you take on pressures you were never created to cope with. You have allowed your husband to escape his responsibilities, and your family structure will begin to deteriorate.

Finally, we must say that this life-style of submission is extremely difficult to live for anyone who has not submitted her/himself to the Lord Jesus as we have mentioned above (Ephesians 5:21).

The husband's role

The husband's role is a more demanding and heavier responsibility to carry than that of the wife. Listen:

*'Husbands, love your wives, just as Christ loved the church
and gave himself up for her to make her holy, cleansing her
by the washing with water through the word, and to
present her to himself as a radiant church, without stain
or wrinkle or any other blemish, but holy and blameless. In
this same way, husbands ought to love their wives as their
own bodies. He who loves his wife loves himself. After all,
no-one ever hated his own body, but he feeds and cares for
it, just as Christ does the church – for we are members of
his body. For this reason a man will leave his father and
mother and be united to his wife, and the two will become
one flesh. This is a profound mystery – but I am talking
about Christ and the church. However, each one of you
also must love his wife as he loves himself, and the wife
must respect her husband.'*   (Ephesians 5:25–33)

This passage has been quoted at length to show the
heaviness of the man's task.

A young man once met with his pastor to explain a
problem. He said, 'Pastor, I'm afraid I love my wife too
much. She is always on my mind.' The pastor asked, 'Son,
would you be willing to die for her?' 'Well,' the man
answered slowly, 'that's something I'd have to think
about.' 'Then, young man, your problem is not that you
love your wife too much. You don't love her enough.'

This is the problem with many men. They all like to
quote the Scripture to their wives: 'The Bible says "Wives
submit to your husbands."' They demand submission,
but they fail to love in the way the Bible wants them to
love their spouses. If you want your wife to submit herself
to you the way the Bible commands her to, you've got to
love her in like manner. Your love for her must be strong,
it must be stable, and always seeking nothing but the
highest good for the one you love. It is a love expressed in
word and action.

As the head of your wife, your primary task is to love the
way Christ loves. You lead your home in love. You teach
in your home with love. You are the priest in your home,
so you intercede for your home in love. You protect your
home with love. You provide for your home with love.

You counsel in your home with love. You encourage in your home with love. You discipline in your home with love and you care for your home with love. That is what it means to be a man and to be a husband in the biblical sense.

H. Sex

As we have said above, in the definition of marriage, sexual union is the consummation of that exclusive hetero-sexual covenant between the husband and wife. Yes, the secular world has perverted it through pornography, vulgar languages, and sexual crimes. Notwithstanding, it remains purely a gift of God. The Bible says:

> *'Every good and perfect gift is from above, coming down from the Father of the heavenly lights, who does not change like shifting shadows.'*   (James 1:17)

Sex is one of the good and perfect gifts that come from God. However, there is nothing that God gives to man that could not be misused through the devil's influence. Day to day we witness the misuse of the spiritual gifts. But we still believe that these gifts are indispensable for the growth of the Church. Sex is likewise vital for a marriage to be blissful. Hence, it is something to thank God for rather than feeling loathsome at the mention of it.

Sex and holiness aren't antithetical. The holy God who created man, *'male and female'* (Genesis 1:27) in the beginning, intended the idea of sex to be a part of holy matrimony. Sexual experience outside marriage however, is a sinful act; for the Scripture exhorts:

> *'Marriage should be honoured by all, and the marriage bed kept pure, for God will judge the adulterer and all the sexually immoral.'*   (Hebrews 13:4)

The topic of sex is a very big one which we cannot cover in detail at all in this book. For the people who are entering marriage and those who are married and want to improve their physical relationship, we recommend books such as *The Act of Marriage* by Tim and Beverly

La Hay, which is a very detailed book written from both a Christian and medical point of view.

☞ For the husband only

You need to educate yourself as much as you can about this subject in order to bestow upon your wife the greatest lovemaking experiences possible for both her benefit and your own. There is a saying that 'A woman is the most complex creature on earth.' Such a fact should encourage you to study to know many things about her, such as what her erotic needs are and what marriage itself truly means to her. Be curious and find the way to satisfy your curiousity about what turns your wife on for sex. Practise self-control. Paul says,

> *'Each of you should look not only to your own interests, but also to the interests of others.'*   (Philippians 2:4)

Many husbands often fail to take their wives's own sexual needs into consideration since their own can be satisfied in a few seconds. This leaves the wife feeling she is being used, rather than being loved.

☞ For the wife only

Nearly every wife genuinely wants to succeed in this important area of marriage, but too many just don't know how to proceed. We therefore reckon that a little suggestion given herein will be helpful. In woman's sexual thinking pattern, three areas are very important:
(a)   what she thinks about lovemaking;
(b)   what she thinks about herself; and
(c)   what she thinks about her husband.
Her attitude toward these will determine her success or failure.

(a) What she thinks about lovemaking

Many married women have many false conceptions of sex. To some, it is 'dirty' and 'evil' and to others, it is 'for masculine enjoyment only.' To others still, 'it is solely for bringing children into the world.'

Among these women was a woman whose marriage was

arranged by her parents some years ago. She found herself petrified of sex on her wedding night. When her embarrassed husband, who was twenty years older, brought her to their wedding bed, 'he (the lady complained) stripped me naked and raped me in my own bed. I fought and screamed to no avail. My virginity was gone and I cried for three days. I have hated sex faithfully for thirty-five years.' She therefore concludes: 'As far as I'm concerned, marriage is just legalized rape.' Can you see the awful consequence of a wrong conception of lovemaking? When the head of the woman had been computerized with such information about sex, the result will always be failure in bed.

(b) What she thinks about herself

Self-rejection is one of the most common maladies of our day. Men fret about their penis being too small or too soft; women worry about having miniature-sized breasts or being undersized. Anxiety over one's ability to function sexually is the primary cause of sexual malfunction. In other words, your organs themselves are not of primary importance, but what you think about them and yourself.

(c) What she thinks about her husband

If you gripe and criticize your partner in your mind, before long your love will die. If however, that negative mental habit is replaced by thanksgiving for the positive characteristics in your partner's life, love will blossom as surely as night follows day. Love is the result of thinking wholesome thoughts about one's partner. Listen to what brother Paul says:

> '. . . *Whatever is true, whatever is noble, whatever is right, whatever is pure, whatever is lovely, whatever is admirable – if anything is excellent or praiseworthy – think about such things.'*   (Philippians 4:8)

Another hint to give to the wife is this: first, **remember that men are stimulated by sight**. I've been thinking over the directive that our Lord gave to men:

> *'But I tell you that anyone who looks at a woman lustfully has already committed adultery with her in his heart.'*
> (Matthew 5:28)

What about a woman who looks at the man lustfully? The statement wasn't directed to women because men are quickly stimulated visually, and the most beautiful object in a man's world is a woman. Many women counsellors urge wives to make the daily homecoming of their husbands the most significant time of the day. By bathing, fixing their hair, and putting on fresh attire, they are prepared to give their husbands an enthusiastic welcome home each night. A contented husband is one who is assured that the loveliest sight of the day greets him when he opens the door at night.

Another point: **never nag, criticize, or ridicule**. Nothing turns a man off faster than motherly nagging and criticism or ridicule of his manhood. No matter how upset a wife may become, she should never stoop to such conduct, or she may jeopardize a beautiful relationship.

Observe daily feminine hygiene. This advice is necessary for two reasons: first, according to the experts in gynaecology, in some women the vaginal fluids, especially those which have dried on the outside, can emit a strong odour unless she bathes regularly; and second, she may become immune to her own body smells. In this day of various special soaps, lotions, and deodorants, body odours should never be a problem.

Communicate freely. Do not assume that your husband knows everything about sex. Tell him what he should do to turn you on during the foreplay, and how you feel all along. Do not be afraid to guide his hands to areas of your body that give you pleasure. Unless you do this, he will always remain ignorant about you.

Finally, **do not use sex as a weapon against your husband**. The result is always catastrophic. Listen to what Paul says:

> *'The wife's body does not belong to her alone but also to her husband. In the same way, the husband's body does not belong to him alone but also to his wife. Do not deprive*

each other except by mutual consent and for a time, so that you may devote yourselves to prayer. Then come together again so that Satan will not tempt you because of your lack of self-control.'   (1 Corinthians 7:4–5)

I. Be Independent of In-laws

I remember in our last week of study at London Bible College, after three years. The Principal, Dr Peter Cotterell, assembled all the graduands and addressed us. He spoke to us on many subjects, but one of the topics that stuck in my memory is **the reaction of some of his staff.** He warned us that we should not be surprised when some lecturers withdraw from us or behave strangely towards us in these last days. That is the only way they know they can help themselves after the relationship of three consecutive years. They are only missing us! Just imagine, these are teachers, friends and advisers. And if they have spent only three years with us and they reacted (as some of them actually did) in such manner, how much more one's parents who have been involved in our lives since birth? So let us look at the possible reactions of our parents.

Reactions of our beloved parents

Parents react to the loss of their beloved daughter or son in various ways. Sometimes the reaction may be over-protective especially when one is the only child. They will be tempted to criticize the young marriage partner and assume that their child is not being as well looked after as he or she was at home. A young wife is frequently accused of not feeding her husband properly or not cleaning the house properly, and a husband may be considered to be a bad provider if he is not ambitious in his job.

Lessons from the creation order

'For this reason a man will leave his father and mother and be united to his wife, and they will become one flesh.'
(Genesis 2:24)

The importance of 'leaving' and 'cleaving' can be seen in the fact that this verse reappears in the New Testament four times: in Matthew 19:5; Mark 10:7; 1 Corinthians 6:16; and Ephesians 5:31. The idea of uniting with, 'cleaving', is an interesting one. The Hebrew word that is used, *dabaq*, appears again in Job, in a passage that speaks about the crocodile. Listen:

> *'His back has rows of shields tightly **sealed** together; each is so close to the next that no air can pass between. They are **joined** fast to one another; they **cling** together and cannot be parted.'*   (Job 41:15–17)

The newly wedded couple, the in-laws and the friends must learn the lesson here that this is what marriage is all about – it is about **leaving**, **cleaving and becoming**. When we say 'leaving', this is more than something geographical, i.e. moving away from the parental home, but something that is psychological. It is to break away from the original parental ties. This is where many married couples fail. Socially, they enter into a wedding ceremony, but psychologically they are not prepared to move from one relationship to another. The word 'leave' however, does not suggest that a couple now abandon their parents and show no more concern or interest in them. What it means is that the couple moves out from under the authority of their parents to establish for themselves a new authority structure. If you are the husband and you want to maintain an emotional authority relationship with your parents, you will feel inadequate as a leader. Likewise, if you are the wife and you fail to make a psychological break with your parents you will certainly feel insecure and unable to trust your husband's leadership.

The word 'cleave' means a commitment to hold on and advance against every force or threat which would seek to divide the loyalties and fidelities of the marriage union.

A minister friend of mine, Samuel (not his real name), always thanks the Lord that he and his wife have a proper enlightenment on this subject of 'the creation order', otherwise, he said, his marriage would have collapsed long ago when his sister-in-law, Susan (not her real name), one day came with full force to undermine their loyalty and commitment to their marriage and each other. Like a demon-possessed woman, Susan came in and started abusing Samuel verbally, pointing fingers at him and calling him names, all because they would not allow her to rule their home as she wanted. On the second day, she telephoned and demanded from Ruth that she choose whether she wanted to be on her side, or Samuel's. Susan is a funny breath that attempted to come between the crocodile's back of Samuel and Ruth's marriage. It wasn't possible for her simply because it was made of rows of shields, fastened together and hard as stone. Is your marriage like that?

J. Little Foxes that Ruin the Vineyards

> 'Catch for us the foxes, the little foxes that ruin the vineyards, our vineyards that are in bloom.'
>
> (Song of Solomon 2:15)

Like the love of these lovers in the Song of Solomon for each other, and the surpassing beauty of the woman compared to that of the other girls in Jerusalem, your marriage or matrimonial home is a vineyard. If you have a blissful marriage, there is joy there, you do not lack peace in your home, you understand one another, you are blessed with godly children, and you are growing up spiritually. Be watchful, the foxes are nearby. What do we mean by foxes? Anything that is dangerous to the peace and stability of the people of God. Anything that acts as an enemy of God and of his people is described as 'fox' or 'jackal' in the Bible. The false prophets are foxes (Ezekiel 13:4), the persecutors are foxes (Luke 13:32) and sin as well.

In your matrimonial home, be vigilant and be on your guard against those hurtful and disturbing elements that always seek to creep in. Such as little jealousies, little coolnesses, enstrangements, pride, being economical with the truth, unhelpful jokes, an uncooperative attitude and much more. You may regard them as little, but remember, little foxes are capable of destroying a whole vineyard, therefore catch them.

The word 'ruin' in this passage is very strong in Hebrew. It means 'to brutally destroy' and that's what foxes do to vineyards. They are brutal in nature, so don't be careless about your marriage. Always go on your knees and ask Christ to 'catch for you the little foxes that may seek to ruin your vineyards.' But that is when we translate this verse in an imperative mood; we say 'catch for us' in our prayer for we cannot catch them ourselves. However, if we translate it in a cohortative mood, we say 'Let us catch them, the little foxes...' Can you see the sense of it? There are some foxes or destructive forces in your matrimonial home that you will not be able to capture yourselves unless Christ does it for you. But there are many unhelpful habits in marriage that you do not need to pray about but just do it yourselves. With the spirit of agreement between you two, catch them. Throw them away. The author of Hebrews writes:

> '...let us throw off everything that hinders and the sin that so easily entangles...' (Hebrews 12:1)

References

1. F.H. Palmer, *The New Bible Dictionary*, pp. 710–711
2. Mary Batchelor, *Getting Married in Church*, pp. 9–11 (emphasis mine)
3. Ed Wheat MD and Gay Wheat, *Intended for Pleasure: Sex Technique and Sexual Fulfilment in Christian Marriage*, p. 32
4. Ed Wheat MD and Gay Wheat, *Intended for Pleasure: Sex Technique and Sexual Fulfilment in Christian Marriage*, p. 32
5. Selwyn Hughes, *Marriage as God Intended*, p. 49
6. Peter Cotterell, *Look Who's Talking!* p. 105
7. Julie Reeves, *For Better, For Worse?* p. 15
8. Selwyn Hughes, *Marriage as God Intended*, p. 37
9. Woodrow Kroll, *Is There a Man in the House?* p. 43

Chapter 5

Things Fall Apart:
Divorce and Remarriage

We must confirm right from the beginning of this subject that it is not an easy one to deal with. Divorce is a very puzzling subject for all Christians. For instance, can Christians ever encourage other Christians to divorce and remarry? Can the church offer such encouragement? Can it bless those remarrying? Can it bless the new vows?

Another major reason that makes this subject a very difficult one to deal with is that the law of the land stands on the one side, and the law of God stands on the other. According to the law of God, marriage is a lifelong agreement; divorcement is a stranger to it. Although some have argued that if lifelong marriage is a norm, it is certainly a norm with exceptions. Thus Helen Oppenheimer said in her article on Divorce in *A New Dictionary of Christian Ethics*:

> 'There are many possible grounds for divorce, from falling out of love to cruelty. The most universal ground has been adultery, especially a wife's adultery, which is felt by nearly all societies to cut at the root of marriage and family life.' [1]

The law of the land on the other hand, changes according to the situation, culture or society. To follow such a law and put aside the law that is settled eternally in heaven makes this subject of divorce as puzzling as it is today. I will soon explain fully what I mean by this. To get a clear idea of what divorce is, let us first of all look at what it is not.

What Divorce is Not

(a) Divorce is not a separation

By 'separation' we mean separation from bed and board. When the couple agree together to live apart; to avoid going out together as husband and wife, perhaps as a 'cooling period'. It is very serious and the Bible by no means encourages a Christian couple to do it. Yet, it is not divorce.

(b) Divorce is not nullity

By this we mean an attempted marriage that never was real. Take the marriage of convenience for instance. The contract was from the first an invalid one. The dissolution of it therefore, cannot be regarded as divorce.

What Divorce Is

If the biblical concept of marriage as stated above, is:

> 'an exclusive heterosexual covenant between one man and one woman, ordained and sealed by God, preceded by a public leaving of parents, consummated in sexual union, issuing in a permanent mutually supportive partnership, and normally crowned by the gift of children,'

then, divorce is a repudiation of it. Intended to free the parties, in order to make the same commitment to someone else.

From these definitions of marriage and divorce, two things are clear. First, that marriage was instituted by God, and it is ideally indissoluble. Secondly, that divorce is a human institution.

Now the question is: what led man to repudiate what God has instituted for his (man's) own personal advantage? The genesis of the matter can be traced back to the book of Genesis. In Genesis 2:23–24 it is clear that marriage was instituted by God **before** the fall of man. After the fall, however, we see the effect of sin which is a radical breach of relationships: the breaking of the relationship between God and the man whom he had made in his own image; the breach of the relationship between Adam and the ground from which he was made (*'adam* and *'adamah*), since he has to go through painful toiling now before he could eat; the strange gap that now appeared in the marital relationship between Adam and Eve, as we see man here blaming his wife for what has happened to them; and the crack in the relationship between two brothers, for Cain slew his brother – Abel. Can you see how everything has radically deteriorated? That is the cause of divorcement in general.

There may be many other 'specific' reasons, as Selwyn Hughes declares:

> 'There are about twenty to thirty specific reasons why marriages break apart, and many of these can be narrowed down to one basic reason – self-centredness.'[2]

In general, though, sin is the root of it, of which self-centredness is supreme.

There is no question about it, God *'hates divorce'* (Malachi 2:16). He hates what occasions every divorce. He hates the results that often bounce on the children and the injured parties of a divorce.

> 'Marital breakdown is always a tragedy. It contradicts God's will, frustrates his purpose, brings to husband and wife the acute pains of alienation, disillusion, recrimination and guilt, and precipitates in any children of the marriage a crisis of bewilderment, insecurity and often anger.'[3]

And that is why we Christians, particularly the pastors, must engage in a thorough biblical teaching on marriage and reconciliation.

Do you notice that when our Lord Jesus was confronted by the Pharisees with the question about the grounds for divorce, he referred them instead to the original institution of marriage? We, likewise, if we allow ourselves to become preoccupied with divorce and its grounds, rather than with marriage and its ideals, we lapse into

Pharisaism. For God's purpose is marriage, not divorce, and the gospel of our Lord is good news of reconciliation.

The Permissive Bill of Divorcement
(Deuteronomy 24:1–4)

In this Old Testament passage we see that a divorce was permitted. A man may give divorce certificate to his wife on the ground of *erwat dabar* in Hebrew. The actual meaning of this word is very difficult to know, but literally, it is the nakedness of a thing. Something indecent, something shameful. This is not necessarily referring to adultery, because death is the penalty for such a sin, but some immodest exposure or unwomanly conduct. This passage was meant to discourage the easy transfer of a woman from one man to another which resulted in the defilement of the woman. This bill then elevates the status of women. But the bill has been misinterpreted by some schools of thought. For instance, while Shammai says 'a man may not divorce his wife unless he has found unchastity in her, for it is written, "Because he has found in her indecency in anything,"' the Hillel school says 'he may divorce her even if she spoiled a dish for him, for it is written, "Because he has found in her indecency in anything."'

Now let us go to the New Testament and see what Jesus says about it.

> *'It has been said, "Anyone who divorces his wife must give her a certificate of divorce." But I tell you that anyone who divorces his wife, **except for marital unfaithfulness**, causes her to become an adulteress, and anyone who marries the divorced woman commits adultery.'*
>
> (Matthew 5:31–32)

> *'I tell you that anyone who divorces his wife, **except for marital unfaithfulness**, and marries another woman commits adultery.'* (Matthew 19:9)

This is Matthew's own account. But now let us look at the Mark and Luke's accounts of the same topic.

> *'He answered, "Anyone who divorces his wife and marries another woman commits adultery against her. And if she divorces her husband and marries another man, she commits adultery."'*   (Mark 10:11)

> *'Anyone who divorces his wife and marries another woman commits adultery, and the man who marries a divorced woman commits adultery.'*   (Luke 16:18)

When you put these three accounts in parallel, you see that the exception clause, 'adultery', appears only in Matthew. Let us ask: did Matthew insert the clause into the account because of the kind of people he was writing to? Or did an early editor insert it into the Matthew's account? We may not know, except to say that if Matthew had inserted it, it is still a good job, for adultery violates the covenant of companionship by introducing another party into the picture. Divorce on the ground of adultery in that case then, is **permissible**, but not mandatory. But according to Mark's and Luke's account, Jesus leaves no room at all for divorce. He regards Genesis 2 as the basic passage for the institution of marriage with death as the only cause for separation. He regards Deuteronomy 24 as a reluctant permission due to human stubbornness rather than divine intention.

By the time Paul was writing to the Corinthians, the situation had changed from that in which our Lord was answering the Pharisees' question. There were two groups in the Corinthian church involved in this matter: to the first group, Paul, like Jesus, does not leave any room for divorce for they are Christians. Listen:

> *'To the married I give this command (not I, but the Lord): A wife must not separate from her husband. But if she does, she must remain unmarried or else be reconciled to her husband. And a husband must not divorce his wife.'*
> (1 Corinthians 7:10–11)

But in verse 12 Paul was addressing a different people whom Jesus did not address, namely, the mixed partners. Paul's response to this situation is that the Christian party must do everything in his power to safeguard his marriage. If the unbelieving party would not, however, Paul used a permissive imperative *'let him separate.'* The Christian partner should not force his/her partner to remain with him/her if the unbeliever feels he has to leave. The Christian should feel free. If the unbeliever were forced to live with the believer, there would be no peace in the home.

The question remains: A brother or sister who has now been divorced by his/her unbelieving partner but is too young to remain unmarried for the rest of his/her life, can he/she remarry again? What does the church say to that? What would you do as a Pastor whose member is in such a situation? What would be your response as a Christian friend to that brother/sister? John Stott's view is helpful here. He writes:

> '... before any church service for the marriage of a divorced person is permitted, the church must surely exemplify its adherence to the revelation of God in two ways. It must satisfy itself first that the remarriage comes within the range of the biblical permissions (that means, divorce and remarriage are not in the original plan of God. He did not command it, but he did permit it because of the stubbornness of man's heart.), and secondly that the couple concerned accept the divine ideal of marriage permanence.' [4]

Once this happens, the church service could not with integrity be identical with a normal marriage ceremony. On the same issue, John Stott explains:

> 'We may on occasion feel at liberty to advise the legitimacy of a separation without a divorce, or even a divorce without a remarriage, taking 1 Corinthians 7:11 as our warrant. But we have no liberty to go beyond the permissions of our Lord. He knew his Father's will and cared for his disciples' welfare.' [5]

References

1. Helen Oppenheimer, *A New Dictionary of Christian Ethics*, p. 160
2. Selwyn Hughes, *The Christian Counsellor's Pocket Guide*, p. 29

3. John Stott, *Issues Facing Christians Today*, p. 259
4. John Stott, *Issues Facing Christians Today*, p. 277
5. John Stott, *Issues Facing Christians Today*, p. 277

Chapter 6

Recovering the Lost Wine

Coming to the last chapter of this book, we aim to look at the situation with many couples in the Church who are not actually divorced, but live together under the same roof as if they were ordinary tenants. The love that unites a husband and wife together has vanished from their marriage. All what they have in common now is just the piece of paper on which they signed their promises to one another and to which some witnesses appended their signatures. Nothing more. They feel nothing for each other except anger, hatred and bitterness. No love, no joy. No security, no respect. No plan, no progress. No peace, no prosperity. The gloomy days have now replaced the past times of bloom.

As David wept and was distressed over the burnt city of Ziklag while all his wives and children had been taken as plunder, so these couples weep and mourn every day and night, with only one song coming over and over again from their lips: 'We no longer see our symbols and who can say how long this will last?' We want to use the experience of David at Ziklag to encourage these friends, to look up to Jesus for, *'he heals the broken-hearted and he binds their wounds'* (Psalm 147:3).

David Encouraged Himself in the Lord

There are some edifying lessons we may learn from David's experience in Ziklag. Saul had driven him out of his country. The Philistines had sent him away from their camp with words of contempt, saying: 'What are these

Hebrews doing here?' His family had been taken away captive. To make matter worse, his own familiar friends threatened to stone him. This was a time of trial for David, for he has lost a lot and hence, he was distressed.

Ziklag means 'enveloped in grief'. So David was, that day. He was wrapped or enfolded with grief. But at this time of disquietude, he believed that God can and will bring light out of darkness, peace out of trouble and good out of evil. Therefore he, the Bible says: '...*encouraged himself in the* LORD *his God*' (1 Samuel 30:6).

A couple of months ago, as we just finished our night vigil, a lady called me aside and said, 'Pastor, you need to pray fervently that God will save my home (matrimonial home). There is fire burning extremely low there now. For the last four months my husband has not slept in the same room with me. When he comes back at night, he will not eat whatever food I give him. At bedtime, when I go to my room he sleeps on the chair in the living room. I think my marriage is crumbling. I'm telling you this because I do not know to what length I can let this go on. But come what may, I believe God is in control.'

All glory to God, after many weeks of prayer and counselling with this couple, they've started living happily together again. But what I admire most in this woman is that while the husband may have given up, she trusted God. She wrote prayer requests to churches asking them to do just one thing for her: 'pray that God will save my home.' And in the end, God did save it.

In situations like this, the first thing a Christian should do is to encourage him/herself in the Lord. That means he should not let Satan undermine his trust in the Lord. To keep on believing that his/her life is in his Father's hand and not to lose the sense that when he weeps, Jesus weeps with him/her too. Listen to what the Bible says:

> '*Cast all your anxiety on him because he cares for you.*'
> (1 Peter 5:7)

Turning the pages of the Bible and kneeling down to pray in such a situation becomes a heavy burden. But do not quit. When the devil has successfully undermined one's strength, then he concludes, 'there is no need for prayer any more.' 'Why bother praying about such and such matter again?' 'It is too late now.' Such are the schemes of the devil. If Satan cannot destroy, he will disturb. If he cannot break your neck, he attempts to break some important bones in your body. But look at him as a defeated foe and encourage yourself in the Lord.

> *'He gives strength to the weary and increases the power of the weak.'*   (Isaiah 40:29)

David Pursued, Overtook, and Recovered All

Having enquired of the Lord whether he should go after the enemies that had brought such a catastrophic experience into his life, and having received an answer of peace from the Lord, David, sad as he was, faint as he was, rose and pursued. We cannot blame all the parties involved in broken marriages, rather we need to stress the fact that in marriage there are certain objects that we have to be pursuing always. Peace, for instance, doesn't come to any relationship automatically, it has to be pursued. Listen:

> *'Peace be pursuing with all men ... '*
> (Hebrews 12:14, *The Emphasized NT*, J.B. Rotherham)

Another translation says:

> *'Run swiftly after peace with all men.'*
> (*The Centenary Translation: The NT in Modern English*, H.B. Montgomery)

The wife needs to run after peace with her husband, likewise the husband with his wife. When there is no peace left in one's marriage that means you are losing some wine and the next thing is to run swiftly after it. You can't just let it go like that. Remember your Lord is the Prince of peace.

Humility is another object to be pursued not just when things go on smoothly, but especially when things are getting out of hand. Peace will not come when we do not clothe ourselves with humility. Listen:

> *'Therefore, as God's chosen people, holy and dearly loved, clothe yourselves with compassion, kindness, humility, gentleness and patience.'*   (Colossians 3:12)

And again:

> *'...All of you, clothe yourselves with humility towards one one another, because, "God opposes the proud but gives grace to the humble." '*   (1 Peter 5:5)

It is a sign of pride and immaturity when you say 'I can't go to him/her first.' One has to come down for the other. It takes lots of grace to cope with a boastful and bumptious partner. But unless we bring it under control, our nature always tends to take wings and fly like eagle. Paul says:

> *'No, I beat my body and make it my slave...'*
>   (1 Corinthians 9:27)

You do this sometimes in order to get your plunders back.

Repentance is another thing. We will say something about forgiveness in a moment. But do you realize the fact that it is very hard to forgive an unrepentant offender? When you have done something damaging to your relationship and you are claiming your right on it, you need repentance, and you have to pursue and overtake it before it is too late. Understand that phrase: 'before it is too late.' In Hebrews 12:16–17 the Bible warns:

> *'See that no-one is sexually immoral, or is godless like Esau, who for a single meal sold his inheritance rights as the oldest son. Afterwards, as you know, when he wanted to inherit this blessing, he was rejected. **He could bring about no change** of mind* (i.e. repentance), *though he sought the blessing with tears.'*

Esau refused the birthright that entitled him to the leadership of the family in preference for a meal (Genesis 25:29–34). Later, after he realized what he had done, and after Jacob had also secured the patriarchal blessing by trickery, he was rejected. His father could not withdraw what he had already given to Jacob. Consequently, it is said that he found no opportunity to repent.

This phrase, *'He could bring about no change of mind,'* according to Howard Marshall, does not mean that Esau found no chance of making Isaac change his mind. Rather God did not give Esau the opportunity of changing his mind and gaining what he had forfeited.[1] Pursue repentance now and overtake it before you find no more opportunity to change your mind.

What is repentance? It is simply a change of mind. Repentance and return will lead to renewal and restoration. If you have failed in your relationship in any way, don't let that failure stop you permanently but look at your failure as a fresh opportunity, not a final defeat. As a Bible interpreter has rightly put it:

> 'Failing to try is the greatest failure anyone can experience, for if you don't make the attempt, you've failed already!'

Perhaps you have failed to keep to the terms of the covenant between you and your partner, you need to pursue repentance and make sure you overtake it.

Finally, lost wine in a marriage relationship cannot be wholly recovered without the sincere forgiveness from one party to another. The word of God exhorts us to

> *'Bear with each other and forgive whatever grievances you may have against one another. Forgive as the Lord forgave you.'*   (Colossians 3:13)

But forgiveness is something that has to be pursued and overtaken. The memories of the hurts that your partner has inflicted on you keep on coming over and over again. This is one difficult aspect of it. The other one is its continuity. You forgive again and again. On hearing this subject of forgiving times without number, the apostles said to Jesus, *'...Increase our faith!'* (Luke 17:3–5). That means they needed greater faith to reach such a standard. In other words, they needed power to pursue and overtake forgiveness.

The result will be recovery of all the lost wine. The Bible says:

> *'David recovered everything the Amalekites had taken, including his two wives. Nothing was missing ... David brought everything back.'*   (1 Samuel 30:18–19)

Don't give up. Whatever is missing in your marital relationship, pursue it, overtake it and recover it. There is hope for your marriage. Listen:

> *'There is hope for a tree that has been cut down; it can come back to life and sprout. Even though its roots grow old, and its stump dies in the ground, with water it will sprout like a young plant.'*   (Job 14:7–9 GNB)

Having done what you ought to do in order to save your marriage, then wait till change will come to your situation. Job says:

> *'If a man die, shall he live again? All the days of my appointed time will I wait, till my change come.'*
> (Job 14:14 KJV)

Change will come to your situation. The question is: can you wait until it comes? Anyone that is undergoing such a trial like yours should exercise faith. Now, there is faith to escape trial and there is faith to endure it. Both need to be exercised in such a situation.

> *'Blessed is the man who perseveres under trial, because when he has stood the test, he will receive the crown of life that God has promised to those who love him.'*
> (James 1:12)

Reference

1. Howard Marshall, *Kept By The Power of God: A Study of Perseverance and Falling Away*, p. 150

Bibliography

Batchelor M., *Getting Married in Church*, Lion Publishing Plc, 1979

Cotterell P., *Look Who's Talking!*, Kingsway Publications Ltd, 1984

Hughes S., *Marriage as God Intended*, Kingsway Publications Ltd, 1983

Hughes S., *The Christian Counsellor's Pocket Guide*, Kingsway Publications Ltd, 1982

La Haye T. and B., *The Act of Marriage*, Marshall Pickering, 1976

Oppinheimer H., 'Divorce' in *A New Dictionary of Christian Ethics*. Eds J. Macquarrie and J. Childress, 1986

Reeves J., *For Better, For Worse?*, Triangle SPCK, 1986

Stott J., *Issues Facing Christians Today*, Marshall Morgan & Scott, 1984

Wheat E. and G., *Intended for Pleasure*, Scripture Union, 1993